Pet Cats

Cecelia H. Brannon

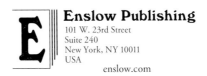

Enslow Publishing

101 W. 23rd Street
Suite 240
New York, NY 10011
USA

enslow.com

Published in 2017 by Enslow Publishing, LLC.
101 W. 23rd Street, Suite 240, New York, NY 10011

Library of Congress Cataloging-in-Publication Data

Names: Brannon, Cecelia H., author.
Title: Pet cats / Cecelia H. Brannon.
Description: New York, NY : Enslow Publishing, 2017. | Series: All about pets
 | Audience: Grade 4-up. | Audience: Pre-school, excluding K. | Includes bibliographical references and index.
Identifiers: LCCN 2015045249| ISBN 9780766076044 (library bound) | ISBN 9780766076273 (pbk.) | ISBN 9780766075863 (6-pack)
Subjects: LCSH: Cats--Juvenile literature.
Classification: LCC SF445.7 .B73 2017 | DDC 636.8--dc23
LC record available at http://lccn.loc.gov/2015045249

Printed in Malaysia

To Our Readers: We have done our best to make sure all website addresses in this book were active and appropriate when we went to press. However, the author and the publisher have no control over and assume no liability for the material available on those websites or on any websites they may link to. Any comments or suggestions can be sent by e-mail to customerservice@enslow.com.

Photos Credits: Cover, pp. 4–5 ajlatan/Shutterstock.com; p. 1 cath5/Shutterstock.com; pp. 3 (left), 14 hannahdarzy; pp. 3 (center), 12 Irina Kozorog/Shutterstock.com; pp. 3 (right), 10 Africa Studio/Shutterstock.com; p. 6 panpilai paipa/Shutterstock.com; p. 8 Nataliia Iliuk/Shutterstock.com; p. 16 olena2552/Shutterstock.com; p. 18 Little JO/Shutterstock.com; p. 20 BestForSell/Shutterstock.com; p. 22 Lenkaden/Shutterstock.com.

Contents

Words to Know

climb

kibble

litter box

Cats make great pets. They like to play with toys.

When cats are born, they are very small. Baby cats are called kittens.

Cats do not like water, so they do not take baths. They lick their fur to stay clean.

Cats use a special box for their bathroom. It is called a litter box.

Cats must eat every day. They like meat and fish. Sometimes their food is dry kibble. Sometimes it is wet and comes in a can.

Cats have claws. These help the cat climb.

Cats can have fur in many colors. They can be black, white, gray, brown, orange, or a mix of these colors. Some cats do not have fur at all!

There is a special plant that cats love. It is called catnip.

Cats like to sleep. Some of them sleep for 16 hours a day!

Cats make a sound called a purr. This means the cat is happy.

Read More

Meister, Cari. *Cats* (Bullfrog Books: My First Pet). North Mankato, MN: Jump! Incorporated. 2014.

Piers, Helen. *How to Look After Your Kitten.* New York: Wide Eyed Editions, 2015.

Websites

Science Kids!

sciencekids.co.nz/sciencefacts/animals/cat.html

Cats for Kids

cats.org.uk/cat-care/cats-for-kids/about-cats

Index

Guided Reading Level: C

Guided Reading Leveling System is based on the guidelines recommended by Fountas and Pinnell.

Word Count: 154